SUCCESS IS MY VIDEO GAME

Written by:

Diamond D. McNulty

DEDICATION

This book is dedicated to young men and women who have a burning desire to succeed and those who have a limited understanding of success. I know what it's like to be lost in life, and I also know the amazing feeling of having true clarity about becoming successful in life. I wrote this book to give you the ultimate clarity on what it means to become successful no matter where you begin. I also wrote this book for all adults, parents and educators who care about the next generation and are desirous to see them reach their ultimate potential in life. I am right there with you cheering them on as we work together to give the next generation the tools to succeed.

I also want to dedicate this book to me. This book was developed from two decades of research and experience. I've been able to organize and share this knowledge with the world in hopes of helping one million youth and adults create their personal success plan.

CONTENTS

ACKNOWLEDGMENTS

I would like to thank my parents, Londa Gray and Derrick McNulty Sr., for giving me the foundation to build a meaningful life. I started from the bottom and that was perfectly fine because I realize that in one generation, I can affect many generations to come by being obedient to God. I am thankful for the environment that shaped me and provided the challenges I needed to grow and build resilience. I am also thankful that I didn't play it safe. I'm thankful I took the time needed to learn and figure out how to win in this game of life.

To the wonderful women in my life who have supported me on this journey, Carrie Jemii, Nikia Gray, Mercedes McNulty, Rose McNulty, LaKeisha McNulty and Sherri McNulty, I love and appreciate you all.

PREFACE

We all have a starting point to our lives. Some people are born rich and some are born poor but once you understand that your circumstances do not define you, the possibility of winning begins to take root in your mind. A positive and optimistic mindset helps you envision things that are not yet seen and fills you with the ultimate joy and thrill of "what if".

- What if you finish high school? Then what?

- What if you don't finish high school? Then what?

- What if you finish college and choose a great career?

- What if you start a business? What if you don't?

- What if you identify your gift and passions, start a business and never give up? What if you never seek to find your purpose in life?

- What if you never step out on faith? What if you stay fearful for your entire life?

- What if you work hard and never work smart? Labor is limited.

- What if you work smart and find mentors?

- What if you learn financial literacy? What if you don't?

- What if you work-out and become extremely healthy?

- What if you were born poor and become rich… what would that do for your family?

- What if you were born rich and you multiply your family business by 10… what impact would that make in the world or the lives of others?

- What if you act spoiled and entitled? Will you gain genuine relationships or lose great relationships?

- What if you think big, eliminated all distractions and focus on reaching your goals in life?

- What if you set goals and focus on creating the life you desire?

I WROTE THIS BOOK JUST FOR YOU

I intentionally wrote this book for you, and I want you to know that your life is in your hands, so keep it that way. Stay out of trouble, stay away from the wrong crowd, identify the things that motivate you and run after your dreams. I just got back from Australia and New Zealand and it will shock you to know that you can't even enter New Zealand if you have a police record of any kind. I want you to be free to travel the world but this freedom comes with the awareness that there are rules to winning in life.

In the past, it wasn't easy to go from nothing to something and succeed at rapid speed. But today, technology and information is more readily available to provide answers to your pressing questions, all you have to do is seek it, learn it, and apply it to your life so you can develop into the greatest version of yourself.

The difference between where you are and where you want to be is a matter of focused time and execution. If you don't come from wealth or have access to an abundance of resources then you will need to build everything from scratch. To do that you must examine your focus: what do you think about on a daily basis? Are you focused on building relationships or getting opportunities? Naturally, access to resources and opportunities to upgrade your life will expand your mind as you continue on your journey to success but you must ensure that you are positively impacting others as well so that when your name is mentioned or heard, there is a positive response. When people know who you are, what you do, and that you have a positive influence or attitude, they are more likely to offer you opportunities.

Staying focused is a vital key for success. Some people accomplish one thing a year and some people accomplish one thing a day, while I strive to accomplish 10 things a day. That's a big difference between accomplishing one thing, 365 things or 3,650 things in a year. Starting from the bottom requires a laser focus on the things you want out of life. When you know where you are headed in life, you can easily map out the steps to get there and focus on accomplishing your goals.

In this book, I am going to break down the steps to success so that you can understand and identify what you need to do to achieve success. I want you to **win** and I pray that when you do, you give this book to 10 more people and help them do the same thing.

Say with me: "Success is my video game."

Let's get started!

LEVEL 1

SUCCESS IS SIMPLE

To win in life you have to learn the rules. Just like any video game that was created for you to play, every game starts with instructions. I have observed that many people desire to be successful but have neither read the instructions or learned the rules.

Here are the instructions or what I call the fundamentals to success and from there I will teach you how to win in life by making success your video game.

The fundamentals of success!

What is success?

Many people come up with so many answers to this question and it confuses them in the long run. If you do not slow down, define and internalize what success means to you, how can you ever obtain it? I repeat, if you do not slow down, define and internalize what success means to you, how can you ever obtain it?

The definition of **success** is simple, it means **"achieving your goals".**

If I was to ask you this same question a million times then I would be looking for this same answer a million times.

What is success? Achieving my goals.

What is success? Achieving my goals.

What is success? Achieving my goals.

Now, if success means achieving your goals, how many goals do you intentionally set on a daily basis? _____

Many people are honestly setting zero daily goals. I mean intentionally setting them with the awareness of moving them from start to finish. Some people make 2-3 resolutions for the new year but even those resolutions are not achieved most times. Which means that out of 365 days in the year, many people are not operating at their maximum potential. Some people are not even keeping track.

Of course, daily tasks have to be done, but I'm talking about intentional forward progress towards success "achieving your goals". As mentioned earlier, my personal goal is to set 10 goals a day. If I accomplish 10 goals per day intentionally, then I would have accomplished 3,650 goals per year. Now, if you analyze that you will be able to see what intentional goal setting and execution looks like. If you begin to intentionally focus on your daily goals and seeing them through from start to finish, you will be light years ahead of everyone. Since my ultimate goal is obtaining billions, I am aware that I have to be 100x more focused on goal setting, strategic planning and execution than others.

Many people aren't intentionally setting goals, writing them down or checking them off which is ultimately delaying their success. I'm sharing my framework for success with you so that you can see exactly how success looks and become the person who sets and achieves all of their goals.

If you want to go over the introduction to success presentation, please visit the link below and register for the success masterclass.

Visit: www.McNultyInternational.com/SuccessIsMyVideoGame

Use Code: Video-game

Back to business: What are goals?

I want you to take a moment to think about the formation of a goal.

All goals begin as an **idea**.

Therefore, **goals are ideas that you commit to achieving**. The only way an idea can become a goal is through commitment.

I need you to do something for me, **Stop ignoring your ideas.**

Write them down and decide if you really want to accomplish them, then commit to it and see the goal through to completion.

How many ideas do you have on a daily basis? Some people have hundreds of ideas every day.

When the ideas come to you what do you do? Many people ignore them, they say that's a great idea and go back to their day without writing it down. Then they wake up 3 years later and see their idea on TV because someone else took the steps to achieve the goal.

You decide if the idea is worth pursuing the moment the idea drops in your mind. The next thing is to process the steps that will turn the idea into a goal. The first thing you need to do in order to turn an idea into a goal is to:

1. **<u>Commit</u>** to the goal - Commit means to pledge, devote and dedicate.

You commit by first saying I will accomplish this particular idea and boom, it's a goal. If you are an honest person once you commit, you will see it through. Don't be a person who breaks your commitments to yourself or others; how well you keep your commitments will define your character. Also, understand your capacity to complete things so that you do not overcommit to more than you can handle.

Some people talk about their ideas without taking any action and they are soon known as "big talkers" instead of action takers. Be different, be an action taker.

After committing to the idea and transforming it into a goal, write it down and organize it in your phone notes or in a notebook so that you can take the next steps to realizing it. Keep working on it every day until it's accomplished.

GOAL CATEGORIES

Goals can be organized into 4 categories: big, small, short-term, and long-term.

As you write down your goals, take note of the categories they fall under and the completion timeline. Some goals may be small-short term goals which can be completed within a week and others may be big-long term goals that will take time and tracking to complete. Organize your goals accordingly so you can move them forward and gain clarity on how to realize them.

How do you achieve your goals? You create a plan!

A plan is a documented roadmap that leads you from having an idea all the way to completing the goal.

Example: Let's think of 10 obtainable goals, 5 short-term and 5 long-term. Now, create a plan to achieve them. Some plans will be short and simple while others may require you to save money, get a job or get additional help to accomplish. However, you need a plan in order to move your goals forward.

So, what's the plan?

This is where you become very strategic and utilize your critical thinking skills. Can you think through the process of achieving your goals before you start them? Do you know the exact steps to take? Have you accomplished goals in the past and how similar are they to your new goals?

To effectively create a plan, you need several tools to map it out. You can use white boards for brainstorming, you can use a brainstorming notebook (you can get one from our website www.ShopMcNulty.com), and you can use your phone notes or a blank sheet of paper. You may also want to loop other smart people in on the brainstorming process to help you figure it out. Sometimes, you won't have all the ideas to create a plan, so it's great to have a team.

Let's dig into an example of mapping out multiple goals at once. I call this project management because each goal is a full project and you have to learn how to manage them until completion.

If you want to drill deeper into creating your personal success plan, join our success club. For 7th grade to high schoolers, we have the How to

Become a Successful Young Man or How to Become a Successful Young Woman Books. For college students we have How to Become a Successful Young Man or Woman College Edition Books. For Adults we have Success Recovery Book and they all have success clubs for every group to join at www.McNultyInternational.com. Those would be the next books for you to purchase if you haven't already. They contain a breakdown of my success journey and includes a workbook that allows you to map out your own personal success plan.

I've mapped out so many goals in life that as soon as an idea comes to mind as a vision, I am able to organize it in my mind, see through the plan and everything it will take to accomplish it within minutes. It's called muscle memory and strategic planning and as you begin to accomplish goals, you will gain the confidence to move it forward faster and your faith will also get stronger. You will begin to process in your mind how to accomplish things way before you even get started while others stay stuck in the idea phase because they lack this understanding of how to keep moving their ideas forward.

Fear of failure also stops many people from completing their goals. They feel it is safer to live without taking risks but this mindset only guarantees an average life. Don't allow fear to stop you, invest and believe yourself.

After creating the plan, the next step is immediate action. Many people create plans but never take action. A mental model I live by is "instant action". I believe in taking action instantly so that I don't get distracted, discouraged or delayed in my efforts. This mental model helps me eliminate procrastination and accelerate the successes in my life. #InstantAction

When mentors recommend books for me, I buy them instantly, read quickly and apply the lessons to my life, instantly becoming a better version of myself. I also follow-up with them, letting them know I read the book and to thank them for the recommendation. This seemingly "little" gesture shows that you value recommendations and follow-through suggestions, thereby boosting your credibility.

Some people wait one year to buy the books that were recommended, unknowingly delaying their progress and forgetting the next action to take because they never wrote it down in the first place. Successful people watch the actions of others and assess their rate of success based on observed actions. Are you a person who takes instant action? Always think your actions through to ensure you don't tumble down the wrong path.

> *After taking action you must do this important thing: never give up.*

It doesn't matter how long it takes, how hard or how many obstacles, you will triumph. Challenges exist to build your character, faith, and determination to succeed. Just as if you were playing a video game console, keep trying until you beat that level. Keep trying until you succeed in accomplishing your goal. You may have to re-strategize sometimes, but never give up on the ultimate goal.

> **"Anything is possible if you believe in yourself, create a plan, take action and never give up."**
> *- Diamond McNulty*

One final thought to bring everything together!

An idea (committed goal) + a plan + action will eventually produce success. Some successes will be easy, some will be more challenging but once you apply this framework time and time again, you will become a success machine.

Make success your video game and eliminate all distractions.

BACK STORY

I loved video games, it started with Nintendo, Sega and all of the other systems we had as children. But I got a new awareness when my mother brought home our first computer – a Compaq Presario. I remember playing strategic army games on it where I had to conquer land and complete different missions. Winning thrilled me and I became very competitive. As my collection of games expanded, I grew more confident in my abilities to figure out challenges as I was very strategic. That same confidence shifted to my baseball and board games like checkers, and every other game we played as children; I was passionate about winning.

I got a rush as a child whenever we competed against other kids in a foot race running from this line to that line. It was in these early days that I became fueled by obstacles. My mother on the other hand was very supportive of my endeavors and very intentional about placing me in programs that would help me develop my skills so that I had access to more than she did growing up. Her exact words were, "I want y'all to have what I did and more". Needless to say that she is my biggest source of motivation.

What or who motivates you? Who is your biggest source of motivation?

I grew up in poverty inside the low income projects in Chicago and at that time I was unaware of how much there was to life. I followed my daily routine of waking up, going to school and coming home. It's the same daily life for everyone until you imagine better for yourself, step out on faith and commit to your ideas of building something that has never been built before. I am one of eight children, three on my mother's side and five on my father's side. We lived on the Northside of Chicago and on the weekends, I would visit my grandmother's house on the Southside where she had a front yard/backyard and all my other brothers and sisters would join me.

Growing up, I was very observant and could tell the difference in my environments. When I was at home inside the projects, sometimes our elevators didn't work and we had to use the stairs, I noticed people doing illegal activities inside the hallways and more. When I visited my grandmother, it was a totally different lifestyle; she lived in a single family house so we were the only ones inside her home. As I got older, my aunt Sherri would pick me up and take me from the projects to visit her home in the suburbs. She had a pantry full of food/snacks and on Christmas I remember her having so many presents under the tree for my cousins and it inspired me. When I returned from visiting her house to our hallways full of disparity, I told myself I would be rich when I get older, and buy my mother a house in the suburbs. At that time my mindset had shifted. I no longer just wanted to win at traditional video games, I wanted to win in real life and that's when success became my video game.

From that moment, I ensured that I operated at my maximum potential in every job or task that I took on.

I began asking myself... Can I get straight A's in school? Yes! It became my video game. How can I win MVP on the varsity baseball team as a freshman? It became a game to me and I accomplished it.

Every challenge became my video game and I was committed to winning. Every challenge that you face in life I want you to look at them as a video game as well and no matter what obstacles you face, you can succeed. Now that you know the fundamentals to success you can now think through how you can use them to reach your goals in life. Take this time to reflect on what was shared and write down anything that stood out to you on the next two pages.

Success is your video game.

NOTES

NOTES

LEVEL 2
100 YEAR MARATHON

THE RACE OF A LIFETIME

We all have a unique starting point in our lives but in this chapter I want you to focus on the big vision and the true lifespan of the average person. According to the CDC in 2022 the average life span for both sexes are 77.5 years. For males it is 74.8 years and for females it is 80.2 years.

After learning how to create short and long-term goals, taking instant action and creating the next steps, let's carve out that **big dream** or **ambition** you would like to accomplish.

For **example :** My big dream or greatest ambition is to have $120 billion dollars, 170 companies, 12 kids, 1 wife, 1000 acres on each continent and to ensure my elders, siblings and successors are setup for success.

What big dream would you like to accomplish in your life span?

I want you to envision all of life's possibilities for you, your family, your legacy and more. Think about it.

If you were to live up to 100 years, what would it look like?

How many vacations will you take every year?

How many children will you have?

What schools will you attend next?

_____

_____

What type of friends or relationships will you attract?

_____

_____

What's your end goal? What do you want in life?

_____

_____

The goal is for you to connect the dots from where you are to where you want to be in life..

Now that you know the fundamentals of success, I am confident that you can begin envisioning all of life's possibilities and how to achieve them. It doesn't matter if you are currently poor or rich, you can win in life.

If you were to live for a hundred years, what are some things you'd like to accomplish in your lifetime? What's your end goal?

I ask that question because I want you to think, I want you to use your imagination, craft out a preliminary plan for your life. I also want you to be aware that all inventions were created by humans and that you should contribute to the world by acting on the ideas that come to you. On the other hand, I don't want you to think that success is easy, it's not easy but it's simple.

It's simple because there is a formula to it but the actual process may be challenging and it depends on where you start, the available resources, your efforts, the books you read, the access and opportunities you are afforded on your journey and more. Are you up for the challenge?

You are entering the race of a lifetime and now that you are aware that you may have on average, less than 100 years to live, you can properly plan your next steps to success.

One decade at a time exercise:

Below, I've mapped out a typical lifespan of a human being. I want you to list out 3-5 highlights that has happened or will happen for you within these particular decades in your life. If you live past 100yrs old then that's great, plan out how long you believe you will live.

From Birth -10 years old

_____

_____

_____

_____

10 - 20 years old

_____

_____

_____

_____

20 - 30 years old

_____

_____

_____

_____

30 - 40 years old

_____

_____

_____

_____

40 - 50 years old

_____

_____

_____

_____

50 - 60 years old

_____

_____

_____

_____

60 - 70 years old

_____

_____

_____

_____

70 - 80 years old

80 - 90 years old

90 - 100 years old

From: _____ to _____ years old

Now think about this, you've listed out 100 years' worth of highlights but what if someone who listed out 100 years' worth of highlights only lived to be 60 years old. How many highlights did that person get to enjoy? How many did they miss?

I created this exercise to teach you two things:

1. I want you to create intentional highlights every day of your life with those you love, smile, laugh, have fun and do great things but don't wait until 60 years or your retirement to begin living. Although we mapped out 100 years it doesn't mean everyone will live up to 100 years. If you create highlights everyday then you're creating 365 highlights per year and 3,650+ in every decade. Talk about a fulfilled intentional life, so no matter what happens, you have enjoyed yourself. As I mentioned in the first chapter there will be big goals, small goals, big highlights, and small highlights as well. Enjoy them all.

2. Never procrastinate. Create goals every day and execute them as if there is no tomorrow. Maximize the day. For many people there are 24hrs in a day but I like to double that because I work double-time on my goals so I joke and say that there are 48hrs in a day if you really lock-in and execute. There is a sense of urgency needed when it comes to executing every day. Show up every day for yourself and for others and be the best you can be in all areas of your life.

WHY SUCCESS?

Success is the greatest form of fulfillment; it is the cherry on top.

Success is the completion of all things started. I often joke with my team and ask them, "How do you spell happiness?" And they answer, "P.R.O.G.R.E.S.S."

Daily progress which moves you towards success allows you to stay happy because it gives you purpose.

I want you to focus on your **why.** Why is it important for you to succeed in life? Someone may not have the energy to win and it's difficult for them to see **why** they should put the effort to succeed especially when there is a lot of work involved compared to just going to work and returning home.   It is vital that you identify your motivations. If you are unmotivated, uninspired and feel hopeless due to life's circumstances I need you to snap out of it, identify your **why** and hold on to it. You only get one shot at life, maximize it.

Example: For me growing up in poverty was one of my **why**. I had access to seeing what wealth looked like at a young age and was able to compare the life I wanted with my reality at that time. I could taste success and accepted the challenge to make success my video game and run after all my dreams for the rest of my life.

What is your why?

_____

_____

_____

_____

_____

Why do you want to become successful?

_____

_____

_____

_____

_____

Good news and bad news.

Achieving success isn't enough, that's the video game. The world is ever evolving so it's important for us to know that while we are accomplishing our goals, success being the end point of some goals, it's still the beginning of the next big idea. Why? Because goals grow.

GOALS GROW

Goals start off as seeds of ideas but over time they develop as you work on them and blossom into creations. The only constant thing in the world is change, that's why we plan our life's journey, predict certain outcomes and prepare for it. Because we have a limited time on this earth we have to plan for success and accomplish the goals we set out to achieve. Many people are so focused on taking action they forget to plan before and after the goal is completed.

You can create things that will live after you whether it's an invention or a business. If it's a business, you can build it to sell and the next generation can use the money from the sale of the business to expand their ideas as well. Sometimes, the goals you work towards are very special and you want to pass them down as a legacy to your successors, therefore, it is important you think the goal from inception to completion and beyond.

A smart person takes the time to think about the timeline of their goal and creates a strategic plan for executing it. If you are really great then you will do all of that before you even start the goal but always leave room for "what if".

What if certain things don't go as planned? What if they do?

Think of every obstacle and create solutions for them before you encounter them in reality. Make success your video game.

NOTES

LEVEL 3

THE SWEET SPOT

> *"A man's gift maketh room for him, and bringeth him before great men." – **Proverbs 18:16***

This chapter is one of my favorites because it shows you exactly what you have in your hands to achieve success – your gifts. When you finish with "Success is my video game", you will completely understand what success means and how to obtain it as simply as possible.

There is a poem by Maya Angelou titled "Hey Black Child" that reminds me of success because it asks all the questions you should be asking yourself no matter your race. If you haven't read it, I encourage you to look up this poem and review it now.

Ok, now let's get into the steps towards using your gifts so that they make room for you.

STEP 1: IDENTIFY YOUR GIFT

The easiest way to become successful in life is by using your gifts, by operating in your passion and walking in your purpose. The trifecta aka the sweet spot. Many people get confused between their gifts, their passion and their purpose; let me help you clarify them.

- Your **gift** is your natural ability. Things that you do with great ease, almost effortlessly.

- Your **passion** is something you love to do. Things that you would rather do over anything else in the world.

- Your **purpose** is the heartfelt life mission you're committed to pursuing because it bridges your gifts and passion to make a difference in the world.

Can you have multiple gifts? Yes.

Can you be passionate about different things? Yes.

Can you have multiple purposes in life? Yes.

I talk about this in my upcoming book One Vision Manifested - *How to Become a Successful Entrepreneur,* I call it your **MVG** and your **MVP**. Your most valuable gift and your most valuable passion. You want to focus the majority of your efforts on your MVG and your MVP while understanding all of your gifts and passions that you can use to become successful.

Example:

- My most valuable gift is cooking.

- My most valuable passion is teaching others.

- My purpose is to help others succeed.

Because my most valuable gift is cooking, I decided to build a business around that gift. Since my passion is teaching, my business is a combination of the two which makes my work feel like fun.

Why is that? Because I do what I am good at and I do what I love all day, every day. I am in the sweet spot of life (gift + passion).

How: I started my first business as a catering company called Taste of Diamond www.TasteofDiamond.com however, I built a secondary business to teach kids and adults how to cook and eat healthy called Chef Diamond and Friends (www.ChefDiamondandFriends.com).

Purpose: My purpose came to me over time by operating in my gifts and passion. My overall purpose in life is to discover purposeful pathways to success for myself and others, personally and professionally. It dawned on me one morning and I clearly saw how the dots connected. Having this clarity has made my journey easier and I want you to experience it as well, that's why I wrote this book. This book is me operating in my purpose in short, helping others succeed.

Your purpose will come to you over time while operating in your gifts and passion. Because I set goals and accomplish them often, I have developed muscle memory for success. Although my success journey will be a bit different from yours, the underlining framework is the same. Let's map out your sweet spot below.

What is your most valuable gift?

_____

List 3 sub valuable gifts?

1. _____

2. _____

3. _____

What is your most valuable passion?

_____

List 3 sub valuable passions?

1. _____

2. _____

3. _____

What is your purpose in life?

_____

It's ok if you don't know your life's purpose yet. I encourage you to operate in your gift and passions, your purpose will come to you.

In 2021, I gave a speech about GPS (God's pathway to success) which I will sum up in this chapter. You can watch the full video on YouTube. Just look up **_Diamond McNulty – God's Pathway to Success._**

STEP 2: ACTIVATE YOUR GIFTS

Now that we've identified our gifts, it's time to activate them. What do I mean by activate your gifts? Test them.

When testing your gifts you want to try them at home, with your family, volunteering with organizations or some sort of way where it's not costing you or anyone else too much money.

Activating your gifts enables you develop the skills for fine-tuning them as well as a greater passion for the gifts. It shows you where you're headed in life, so pay attention to it.

Example:

I spent a lot of my early years volunteering at the Chicago Youth Programs teaching kids how to cook. In return I got an opportunity to test my gifts. I was also testing them in my highest form of passion, which is teaching. I loved it. Checkout the image of me in the sweet spot in high school. .

15+ years later, I am doing the same thing at a school but now I am being fairly compensated for it. What is this telling you? This is the sweet spot.

List 5 ways you can activate your gifts.

1. _____

2. _____

3. _____

4. _____

5. _____

Join our success club at www.McNultyInternational.com

If you have any issues joining or finding it just send us an email at support@mcnultyinternational.com

STEP 3: DEVELOP YOUR GIFTS

Nowadays it's easier than ever to develop your gifts.

The world is so connected online that achieving success is in the palm of your hands. All you have to do is show up and invest in yourself.

- Take classes in school or online.
- Continued learning
- Join workshops and seminars
- Join book clubs
- Join our success groups

For me, developing my gifts started in high school. I had an opportunity to take up Culinary Arts classes as a major from my sophomore year to senior year as an early vocational pathway. As a senior in high school, I was able to compete for the CCAP culinary competition where I won $24,000 to put toward college. That was huge and I would honestly say taking advantage of that opportunity allowed me to get a head start in my career path. It was also a moment for me to select between a vocational skill and baseball because I was a star player in high school.

> *Making the right decisions and showing up!*
>
> *Two important words, "show up". – Joe Hudson*

Early in my career, I asked Joe Hudson to join me for a meeting and he obliged. During our meeting he said the reason he accepted the invitation is because showing up is extremely important. Wise words from a successful elder that never left me. It bothers me when people don't show up for opportunities. Some opportunities you will never get back and could be the difference in you reaching your goals quicker or hitting them at all.

List 5 ways you can develop your gifts. Don't just think about it; add them to your calendar so you can begin taking action.

1. _____

2. _____

3. _____

4. _____

5. _____

List 5 additional skills that could help your gifts thrive?

1. _____

2. _____

3. _____

4. _____

5. _____

How much money have you spent developing your gifts over the past 5 years?

_____

List 5 books that can help you develop your gifts.

1. _____

2. _____

3. _____

4. _____

5. _____

Personally, I don't listen to the radio. When I drive somewhere, I have an audio book playing in my car.

My goal is to maximize the time I have by absorbing information quicker.

Name 3 people who positively influence you?

1. _____

2. _____

3. _____

At this moment do you believe in yourself?

_____

Is success becoming clearer to you?

_____

Are you ready to take over the world?

_____

Success is my video game and success is now your video game, too.

STEP 4: LEARN TO MONETIZE YOUR GIFTS

Monetizing your gifts is the greatest video game of all time. Monetizing is being able to earn money from your gifts. This is the biggest difference between someone who is working a job vs. someone who understands their gifts can help them make a living. There is always someone looking for great people to help them do what they do best.

Example: Here are a couple ways I monetize my gifts.

1. Hosting cooking classes

2. Create books and other products

3. Catering

4.   Speaking engagements

5.   Host workshops

6.   Get a job in your field of choice.

Shy and insecure people have challenges in this area because it requires you to sell your services or products to strangers and/or present yourself to the world. Selling or presenting anything requires confidence. You need a strong conviction to create something and tell someone you are worthy of their hard earned money. If you are shy or insecure, I encourage you to read a lot of books on selling, practice in the mirror and start by meeting strangers and just telling them what you do. I may appear as an extrovert but I am very introverted and I love my privacy so it took me a while to get comfortable with going live on social media.

I shifted from the idea of "selling my gift" to sharing my God-given gifts with others, thus packaging my gift to make it more appealing. I rarely have to sell to the world; however, I do share my gifts with others and they see the value, so they support my business. Once you develop your gifts you become valuable.

Question:

How valuable are you?

_____

If done right, can you make a minimum of $100,000 per year using your gift?

_____

What is the most money you've made in one hour of work?

_____

I've made thousands of dollars for just one hour of work.

Example: If you are paid $2000 per hour then that equals $4,174,000 that year.

There are people who make $10 per hour, there are people who make $100 per hour and there are people who make $2000+ per hour.

What's the difference between them? One person understands their value, believes they are worth it, has proof to show their worth and can communicate it to the world to generate higher income.

The other person may have a great skill but they may be in the wrong environment where those around them have no interest or cannot afford to pay them their worth or they are unsure of how much to charge for their product or services. They may be uneducated and at the beginning stages of business and are still trying to figure themselves out. Either way, I want you to learn and grow.

We often see people trying to monetize their gifts when they should be activating and developing their gifts. They should be learning and taking classes and courses in business to better themselves but they are so focused on making money vs. perfecting their skills. Once you become really good at what you do, then you can charge what you are worth. Don't rush the process but move forward in a timely manner. Do the work and become the skilled "SME Subject Matter Expert" in your area of expertise. It took me 12+ years of hard work and dedication which turned into working smart by building my relationships and resources. With today's technology you can do it faster.

Learn and grow!

- Learn business

- Learn sales

- Learn marketing

- Learn the difference between products and services.

To learn more about monetizing your gifts pick up my book One Vision - How to Become a Successful Entrepreneur or send me a message. I also have a Future Business Leaders Program where I go deeper into business development. Visit www.McNultyInternational.com to learn more or send us a message at support@mcnultyinternational.com

> *Take your time and do it right,*
> *I want to see you succeed.*
> *– Diamond McNulty*

Q&A

List 5 ways you can monetize your gifts?

1. _____

2. _____

3. _____

4. _____

5. _____

STEP 5: CREATE AN ECOSYSTEM AROUND YOUR GIFTS

Here is where the rubber meets the road and the fun begins. At this point you have learned your value and solidified your foundation. You know how to make money using your gifts and are currently using them in your business or working for another company. Now all you have to do is build on it.

Keys unlock doors: In this phase, I want you to look at doors as the "relationships and opportunities" available to you.

Two of the most important questions to ask yourself are:

1. What keys do I have?

2. Who has the other keys?

You have several relationships that will give you access to certain things and places in this world. You've built bridges and connected with a lot of people in your lifetime. You have keys that will unlock doors for you and others. You also have doors that need to be unlocked for you.

Keys come in the form of people or materials. In this sense, people can provide you access and opportunities. If you read a great book, it may unlock new areas in your mind and open more doors of opportunities.

A key may be a nugget of information that unlocks a part of your brain. A key is a resource or anything that opens doors for you.

A key is a person who opens doors for you as well.

Who or where are the keys to unlock opportunities and doors you need to access new opportunities and levels in life?

List 5 keys that you have access to:

1. _____

2. _____

3. _____

4. _____

5. _____

List 5 doors or opportunities that you need to unlock:

1. _____

2. _____

3. _____

4. _____

5. _____

When I say create an ecosystem around your gifts, I am saying all of these things.

- Show up to the right places

- Surround yourself with the right people, read all the right books and register for educational materials that will benefit you.

- Immerse yourself in a lifestyle of growth and development.

If you come to a door that's closed or if someone doesn't want to give you access to the door, it's okay. Keep your composure and don't force it. Figure out another way.

Remember God is the locksmith.

There is more than one way to get through doors and if the door is permanently shut, build a new house with your own doors. You create an ecosystem around your gifts because no one really has to give you anything. It's an honor and a privilege to receive access, opportunities and blessings from others.

Don't take it personally, go get it!

If someone is extremely successful, you can ask to take them to lunch or ask them to mentor you. It's an honor for someone to give you any of their time so if you do get the opportunity to connect with someone who inspires you, maximize the time.

- Present yourself with a humble heart.

- Don't show up begging for opportunities.

- Show that you are willing to do the work.

- Ask the right questions.

- Don't make your time together all about you, it's double- sided.

- Learn to build that relationship.

Support Your Friends

Last year, I purchased books from friends, a friend who created bracelets, a nutritionist and more. When Christmas came around, I had gifts for everyone around me, so I didn't have to go shopping. Recycle your support if you don't need the product or service. Support your friends, even if you don't need their product or service, someone out there may need it. Every bit of support you show them encourages them to do more.

What happens when you need help but haven't supported anyone in anyway or shared their post?

What happens if they break through and you've supported everything they've done?

Don't support because you're expecting something in return, even if they don't support you back, you will increase the favor pool. That's right, blessing others increases the favor pool in the universe and it will come back in other ways when you need it most. Be a blessing to others without focusing on the return. Do good and good will return to you.

NOTES

LEVEL 4

WIN OR LOSE, YOU LEARN

> *"The man who says he can, and the man who says he cannot are both correct"* - **Confucius**

D o you believe in yourself and in your ability to become successful? I am not talking about with someone's help. If no one offered you any support, opportunities or access to resources could you become successful?

Are you up for the challenge? That's the video game.

It's not counting the success of others around you or getting bitter about what you don't have, it's about being thankful for what you have and making the best of it by working toward what you ultimately want in life.

This chapter is about your perception of winning, losing and learning.

Are you a winner?

Have you ever won before?

How did it feel?

Are you a loser?

Have you ever lost before?

How did it feel?

I love this chapter because it's going to give you an amazing understanding of how to view winning, losing, and learning.

Winston Churchill has an amazing quote that says: **"Success is not final, failure is not fatal, it is the courage to continue that counts."**

Allow me to restructure it as well, **winning is not final, losing is not fatal: it's what you learn throughout the process that counts.**

Don't get bogged down by losing and don't get puffed-up when you win. Success is a journey and on it, you will have many losses and many wins over time. If you get too invested in winning or losing then you're up for an emotional roller coaster. Enjoy every moment, learn and apply all of life's lessons and keep going.

HOW TO WIN

Every game has a cheat code. And yes, the game of success has one too.

The Cheat Code - Soul Searching

On your journey to success you may not always have access to someone who can give you the answers to all the questions you may have, so what's the next best thing? Books. I call it soul searching because someone has spent 40+ years of their life mastering a subject, took all the secrets, organized them into approximately 100 pages of a book and only charges $10 - $20 for the information. That's a cheat code.

Imagine if you identified 100 books of interest for personal and professional development that you wanted to apply to your life and all you had to do is get the books of those great people and read it. How great is that? If I were you I would ask for specific books as gifts from everyone around me. Books are my gift of choice.

Books are worth billions! I mostly read books on personal and professional development only. Some people like to read fiction but to me that's a distraction unless I am intentionally reading for entertainment.

How quickly can you read and apply the information in a book?

This skill of reading and applying will determine the speed in which you can reach greater heights as a person. In school they call it comprehension. Can you comprehend what you are reading or is it hard to understand? If it's hard to understand then you may need additional help.

Here are some solutions for obtaining additional help:

- Ask a parent or guardian to explain

- Do some research

- Get a dictionary and define the terms

- Get a mentor or meet with a teacher who you admire

- Get an audio version

- Watch a movie or video on the topic

Either way find out the best way you learn and get the information.

It's not enough to just buy the book or be gifted a book, you must read it, understand it, and apply the gained information as quickly as possible.

How many books have you read this year?

_____

How many books did you read last year?

_____

How many books will you read next year?

_____

Set reading goals!

Begin to measure your progress and track it, if you don't measure your progress you can't track it. Once you reach a certain age, you may not have adults or friends that will hold you accountable. Be the person to do the work even when others are not around. Develop the habits of tracking your progress and you will begin to see great results because you will hold yourself accountable.

MENTORING MATTERS

Mentoring plays a crucial role in your success. Throughout my entire journey I've had a mentor in every area of my life.

When I was a young man in grammar school, my mentors were doctors and lawyers inside the Chicago youth program.

When I was in High School, I had teachers who mentored me and offered additional support in my success journey.

In college I had bosses who mentored me to be a leader in my career field.

When I graduated college and became an adult, I had family men and other professional men who mentored me on my journey. Some mentors focused on family and friendship, some focused on business, some focused on faith and some focused on financial development. They all aided in my personal and professional development.

DON'T WAIT TO BE GREAT!

DON'T WAIT TO BE GREAT

Many youth think they have to be 30 or 40 years old to achieve great success in life but that's not the case. It really depends on how well you learn success, drill down into your gifts, passion and use tools to monetize what you have. Some kids have the blessing of having parents or other adults who believe in them and are willing to invest in them at an early age and that's wonderful. If you have access to someone who can invest in you or a supportive guardian to guide you it will help you succeed faster. If you learn technology and how to monetize it, then by all means run after your goals.

There are two young leaders I love others to learn about:

1. Mo's Bows

2. Mikaila Lemonade

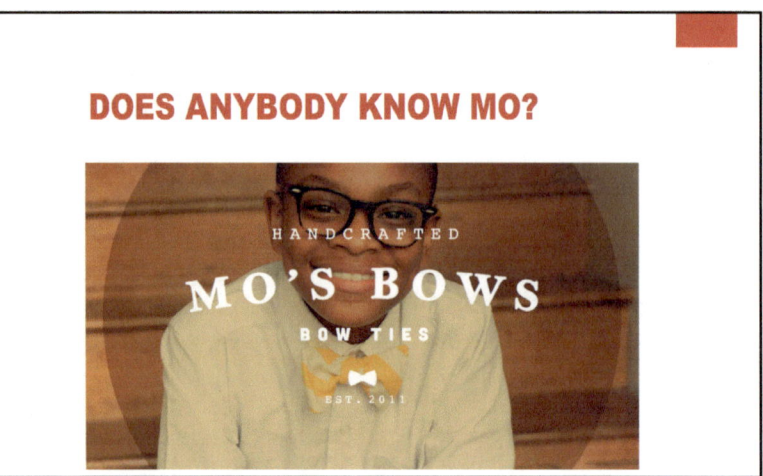

MO'S BOWS

Mo's Bows is a fashion brand that started in 2011 when Moziah Bridges, also known as Mo, was nine years old. Mo wanted to find an accessory that suited his style but couldn't find anything he liked. With the help of his grandmother, who had been sewing for over 50 years, Mo began making his own bow ties using vintage fabrics from her scrap fabric pile. Mo wore the bow ties everywhere and they received so much attention that people asked where he got them. He eventually decided to sell them to friends and family, and the business took off.

Mikaila Lemonade.

Mikaila Ulmer's remarkable entrepreneurial journey began at the age of four when she founded Me & the Bees Lemonade with a mission to save the bees. Over the years, her venture has blossomed into a thriving enterprise, offering her signature lemonade in five delicious flavors and reaching over 1,500 locations. Mikaila's determination and passion caught the attention of the entrepreneurial community when she appeared on the hit TV show Shark Tank, where she secured a deal with the renowned investor Daymond John. Her commitment to her cause and impressive business acumen impressed John and viewers alike. Since then, Mikaila has continued to soar, expanding her product line and forging partnerships with esteemed companies like Whole Foods Market. Her story serves as an inspiration, showcasing the power of youth, innovation, and purpose-driven entrepreneurship.

If they can do great things at a young age, so can you. Don't wait to be great.

I cannot yell this loud enough: **Believe in yourself!** 🗣 Believe in yourself and take action NOW!

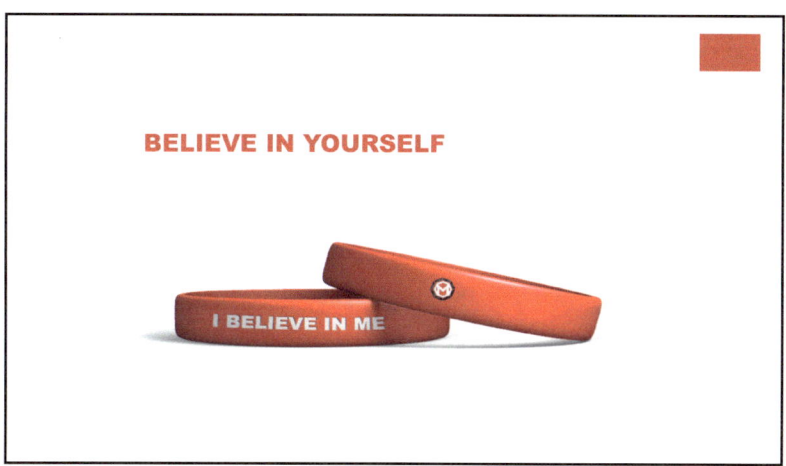

Confidence is the first step to winning.

I BELIEVE IN ME is a wristband I created because I felt it didn't matter if anyone else believed in me, I believed in myself. Remember, it doesn't matter if others believe in you or not, keep believing in yourself.

Here is another quote:

> *"Optimism is the faith that leads to achievement. Nothing can be done without hope and confidence." – Helen Keller*

1. **Hope:** a feeling of expectation and desire for a certain thing to happen.

2. **Confidence:** A feeling of self-assurance arising from appreciation of your own abilities or qualities.

Believing in yourself is not enough; you must do the work as well. You want everything to work in your favor so take the necessary steps and get serious about being great in life.

SUCCEED WITH INTEGRITY

It's extremely possible to succeed at all levels no matter your age, the goal is to win without compromising your integrity. Some people want to win so bad they will do anything to win even cheat and that's not a good thing.

Integrity is doing the right thing no matter who's looking. Always have integrity throughout your journey. Having integrity will sometimes delay your success but that's also a **win**. You have to weigh the things you are willing to compromise but your integrity should never be compromised.

What does having great integrity mean to you?

Give me an example of someone who has compromised their integrity?

_____

_____

_____

Having integrity governs what you do and what you are not willing to do. It's important to be a person with integrity.

STAYING OUT OF TROUBLE

When it comes to succeeding in life, staying out of trouble is half the battle. Many youth just don't realize the importance of staying out of trouble. By staying out of trouble you are ensuring you do not miss out on future opportunities. Having a record of trouble gives you an unfavorable label and could stop you from having certain opportunities as you get older.

Example: As I mentioned earlier, I just traveled to Australia and New Zealand last month and it was very eye opening that the background record of every intending visitor was checked before gaining entrance to the country. I was very thankful I stayed out of trouble as a young man especially growing up in the environment that I did. Another moment where I was excited that

I stayed out of trouble was when I had the opportunity for my business to enter the school system but to gain access to the opportunity, background records were checked. This taught me that no matter how old you get, your background always comes into play in your future. If I had a history of negativity then I would have lost out on a $15 million dollar opportunity. Stay out of trouble!

The wisest thing to do is to learn from the mistakes of others who have gone before you. Those are the cheapest lessons you can obtain. Making the same mistakes others have made could be very expensive and cost you a lot of time, money, relationships, networks and opportunities.

SAY NO TO DRUGS

Nowadays, many of the drugs that used to be illegal are now legal but that doesn't mean you should take them. I want you to stay away from drugs. Drugs are substances that can cause a negative effect on your body and ultimately take you off track from your focus to achieve your goals in life. There are lots of reasons why you shouldn't do drugs but I am not going to drill them down your throat. One of the main reasons why you shouldn't do drugs is because many of them are addictive and if you do them once, you could get hooked, causing you, your family and your future to be in jeopardy. I never understood why someone would spend $20 dollars or more a day on drugs, that's $7300 a year on drugs. If you put that into stocks or even invest into yourself you would get a greater return on that money compared to wasting it.

Doing drugs alters your ability to think properly and to become successful you need a clear mind to observe what is going on around you at all times. Doing drugs is not cool. When you see others doing them, do the opposite and don't be influenced by peer pressure. You have the right to say no to drugs and no one should force you to do anything. If you ever find yourself in a situation where you are uncomfortable and there are drugs around, leave immediately.

Just like in video games, there are many obstacles you need to overcome in life to get to the next level. Unlike video games where you can die and come back to life or restart the game if something happens, you rarely get second chances in real life. You may get another chance but you cannot erase certain things, the best thing is to learn from the mistakes of others and never make those mistakes yourself.

SAY NO TO NEGATIVITY

Negativity can stop you in many different ways, optimism will elevate you on your journey to success but pessimism or negativity will deflate you. Avoid negativity at all costs. I am not saying we live in a world where everything is rosy and smooth but as you ascend to new levels you will begin to see that negativity has no place in success but honesty when properly communicated paves a way to growth and success.

If you want to build great relationships then you must stay positive.

SAY NO TO GANGS

Gangs are organized crime members and their focus usually have a negative impact on the environment and causes harm to others.

Large groups of people who work together for positive efforts are a totally different type of organization and are not addressed by the term "gang or cult".

If you are going to group activities with friends, ensure you are doing it for positive reasons. Street gangs smuggle products and sell illegal drugs and according to the FBI, there are over 33,000 violent street gangs, motorcycle gangs, and prison gangs criminally active in the U.S.

Today, I challenge you to never get active inside the street life, choose the positive route only.

NOTES

LEVEL 5

TAKING OVER
THE WORLD

> *"It always seems impossible until it is done."*
> *— Nelson Mandela*

FAITH

Taking over the world is a phrase I've often used since I was a young man and I believe in it so much that I wrote it on the back of my books. There was only one other time in the world where I heard it besides myself saying it is from a cartoon called Pinky and the Brain. In every episode of the cartoon, the brain spent his entire time developing a plan and working towards it to conquer the world before the episode ended. It must have been a fascinating statement to me as a child because I assimilated it so well that I forgot where it came from. All I know is that I am **taking over the world** and you should too!

As I got older and kept saying that I was taking over the world, many people thought I was out of my mind although I am perfectly fine. I understand why they thought so, it was because I didn't show them how I would actually take over the world. I didn't truly know what I was going to do or how I was going to do it but I believed I would do it.

The fun part is that you have to be semi-delusional while at the same time seeking clarity on how to achieve your goals and dreams. Imagination is something you rarely hear about but there are people in the world who get paid to imagine things. Look up the title of an Imagineer and you can see that Walt Disney alone hires people with imaginations just to envision the possibilities for their company.

Source: glassdoor.com

As I got older, I realized anything is possible if you believe. There are two types of people: those with imagination and those who help build other's visions. Sometimes those with imagination do not know how to build things so they sell their ideas to those who can build it. I started off as a person with great imagination and learned how to become a builder and you can too!

Faith + works! Can you trust in the unknown or do you have to be certain something will work before you get started?

Some people believe in their ideas enough to take action while others have to see it to believe it. Everyone won't have the same faith and it's only when you work towards your goals that you will begin to see things come to life.

Sometimes you will receive your life's mission and you may not know how you will actually bring it to life. Whatever seeds of possibilities that come to you in your imagination are all yours and you have the choice to either bring them to life or reject them. I truly believe everyone has a mission for their life and while some people have accepted theirs, others have limited their potential by rejecting theirs.

I want you to understand that anything is possible. No matter where you start in life, from the bottom of the bottom or at the top of the top, it's possible for you to achieve any and all of your goals if you believe, create a plan, take action and never give up. Dream the impossible dream and bring it to life…make success your video game!

UNDERSTANDING THE WORLD

While I was working as a chef , I understood how the world really functions. I realized the world is geographically broken down into locations.

- Local
- National
- International
- Global

I began to see how local cities were broken down into communities and every community had key elements to function as a community.

Example: Every community had a school, police station, grocery store, etc.

When it came to TV programs certain shows played in certain parts of the world, some on local TV and others on national TV where shows were shown in multiple parts of the united states. I began to drill down into how some celebrities were only local stars, national stars, international stars and some were global icons. I wondered why some stars had global success and why others were limited. It all dawned on me that in the past certain companies were built with access to larger audiences while others did not have access to getting the word out even if they were better than them.

I realized that some companies and wealthy people who had that power and magnitude built their presence and network through generations and are deeply rooted in the world and it would take me, a young man born in poverty, a life-time to truly create something of value for my family and that's even if I had to compete against them and/or others who are already existing. It was at that moment I said, "Wow, I have a lot of work to do if I want to win."

Note: The moment I realized the magnitude of what I was facing I could have easily created an excuse not to pursue taking over the world and moving forward. I could have easily gotten discouraged about winning in life but I changed my mindset and started thinking that I will do it anyway. I figured if I am going to be here on earth then I might as well do what I can to live up to my potential.

Not only did I have to figure out how I was going to take over the world, I was determined to do it no matter the obstacles I faced, which is what I taught you in the first chapter. I had to commit and never give up on my dreams, I had faith that my dreams will come true and the dots will connect as I continue on the journey; looking back at it all, I can proudly say it was worth it.

Over time, I've been able to define what taking over the world means to me and establish a clear vision towards reaching the goal. Without drilling deep into my methodology

Taking over the world is both a personal and professional goal. Personally, I have established my framework as family, faith, friendships, financials and fitness. I have to reach my greatest potential and steward these areas and every day that I work towards them, I am taking over that part of my world. For each of those areas I have roles and goals for myself. Professionally, I have multiple companies I am developing into global businesses which will allow me travel the world as we continue to build in different countries.

Once I committed to achieving the goal of taking over the world, I got straight to **work**.

BECOME A WORKING MACHINE

Now that you understand success, planning, goal setting and life's possibilities, I want you to understand the force you need to put behind doing the work. It's not enough to dream the dream, you must see it through. I cannot tell you how many people get all the way past the planning phase and never take action. Not only do they not take action, you hear all types of excuses why they haven't taken action.

It baffles me when people are aware of the action they are supposed to implement but refuse to do so. You have limited time to build and realize your dreams, don't waste it with inaction. It is the result of your actions that will convince others to believe in themselves. Believing in yourself, your dreams and abilities is something that is non-negotiable. You cannot move forward in confidence with any relationship, goal or endeavor unless you believe in it. If you don't then you are in denial and will ultimately suffer throughout the journey. It's like a friend of mine once said, "walking north and you know you are supposed to be heading south".

Taking action is more than just doing the work; you want to become a working machine. I call it the 48hr rule. I operate as if there are 48hrs in a day vs. 24hrs in a day. I do my best every day to maximize my efforts by doing double the work in half the time while tracking my progress.

A working machine or broken machine, which one are you?

By being a working machine, you acquire the necessary skills to succeed in life. You have to take care of yourself spiritually, mentally and physically. You ensure you are constantly learning and improving by keeping a growth mindset. You have to stay open-minded to the possibilities of life if you haven't reached your big goals yet, but remember you have to be willing to spend every waking moment of your life focused and determined to succeed while making time to enjoy the things that matter throughout the process.

Ever tried turning on your gaming system and nothing happened when you pressed the power button? Some people are system builders or manufacturers of products and some are product consumers. Consumers have zero clue why something isn't working so they need to pay to get it fixed or buy a new one. Now, if you built the system from scratch you will be able to fix the system and you will know what went wrong by simply troubleshooting it. The same thing happens in our lives when we put in the work, step by step, not rushing the process but succeeding in milestones. We learn the ins and outs to what we are building so that if anything happens, we know exactly what to do to get it back on track.

Real success is you taking actions towards a desired outcome and taking note of the process so you can duplicate it later or inspire others to do the same. By becoming a working machine you have to wake up every day laser-focused on executing on the goals you set out to achieve. When your goals are within your sweet spot (gifts, passion, and purpose) working becomes fun and enables you to do twice as much. Many people are working outside their sweet spot and are frustrated; I encourage you to help those around you gain awareness so they can know. Friends don't let friends fail without speaking up.

It has been over 20 years since I first dreamed my big dream and although I have many successes now, I love what I do so much that I don't want to go to bed and I rush to wake up in the morning. I pray you have this type of joy and clarity towards your dreams in life. It took lots of work though and I am not going to say it was easy, I had to overcome a lot of things including myself. I had to personally and professionally evolve into the business leader I wanted to become. That took faith, understanding and most importantly work.

Here are a few things I want you to keep in mind regarding work:

Do what's easy and understand why it was easy.

Do what's hard and it will become easy as well as make you stronger.

Working hard and working smart will make you an expert. If you become the expert and learn leadership, you will be able to build influence and others will want to follow/support you or join your team which multiples your ability to do more.

There will come a time when you have to build a team because the work will be plentiful and you will not be able to do it alone. Take that as a challenge to impact others because your dream can feed a nation and it's your duty to rally everyone around your vision to success. Not everyone will have a vision; you can be a successful person on someone's team as well. Remember:

- Through good times - keep working
- Through bad times - keep working
- Through uncertain times - keep working
- Through learning - keep working
- Through development keep working
- Through high school - keep working
- Through college - keep working
- Through your adult hood - keep working

Learn to love the work.

LEVEL 6

COMPOUNDING
SUCCESSES

> *"Success is the sum of small efforts,*
> *repeated day in and day out." -Robert Collier*

D on't let the work stress you out; take the stress out of your emotions as you work towards your goals. Success is a formula and if you haven't reached your goals just remember to keep going. Many people don't reach their goals because they don't measure their progress. If they did, they will know exactly where they are in the process.

Don't set unrealistic expectations for yourself without a plan to see it through and if you decide to create big expectations then you need to immediately create a plan to bring it to life… Success is simple.

CONSISTENCY

> *"Consistency over long periods of*
> *time creates credibility."*
> *- Diamond McNulty*

Being consistent is a secret to success. Consistency allows you to duplicate any result because you know exactly what was done to achieve them.

Some small successes will happen throughout the journey and those wins are indicators that you are on the right path.

What are success indicators?

- If you are in high school and you pass a math test that's an indicator that you understand the subject and are on the right track.

- If you fail, it indicates that you need to study or seek additional help.

- If you are at your job and someone tips you above the average amount for a tip it's an indicator that you did something well.

- If you never get tips then that's an indicator that you need to find out why.

- If you create a product or service and people patronize you, it is an indicator.

- If you create something and no one buys, it is also an indicator. Take a survey and ask potential clients why they didn't buy so you know what you are doing wrong and what to improve.

Understand the process and appreciate the small wins in the moments when things are not going according to plan. It is the small wins that create the momentum for you to accomplish bigger goals. If you don't appreciate the small wins then you will not find true fulfillment. If you have challenges appreciating your wins, seek guidance from a mentor.

Let me share a secret with you, success is not a one-time accomplishment it is a progressive realization of worthy ideals – it continues! Remember accomplishing your goals are not the end, they grow.

You may have won this years' championship but another competitor is coming for the title next year.

You have to get conditioned and stay conditioned for success. It's a lifestyle.

- You are not done when you graduate high school; you've only successfully accomplished one goal, there are more to follow. What's next? Goals grow so you will either go to college, get a job/career, or start a business and the journey continues. As long as you are alive there is something to accomplish be it your personal goals, professional goals or even helping others achieve their goals. You only have one life to live, there is no room for laziness – there are places to see and ideas to accomplish, so maximize your time.

- Don't waste your time.

If you plan your goals properly, success becomes predictable and you can enjoy the process to achieving your goals. Stress comes when there is no clarity in what you are doing and why you are doing it.

Over time, you will gain major influence if you stay consistent and it will prove to others that you are committed. People love to be around others who know what they are doing, why they are doing it and where they are going.

MICROWAVE SUCCESS

This is not a quick journey where you morph into who you're going to be at the snap of a finger. This is a process. Some successes take time, this means you have to set proper expectations with hopes for miracles, signs and wonders along the way. Microwave success is for those people who haven't read this book and do not understand the journey to really becoming successful.

Those individuals are dreamers only. Some people gain success quicker than others and, in this section, you will learn why.

Some people obtain support from investors and have to share their profits with the investors. Not everyone comes from poverty and some people have the resources to expedite their success.

- Some people focus and execute faster than others.

- Some people enter into certain careers with the right attitude and obtain opportunities quicker because of it.

- Some people study hard and apply everything they are learning faster than others.

There are many ways to expedite your success but you still have to do the work. It is rare to gain opportunities for growth when you don't intentionally embark on the journey to success.

Story: All I have accomplished in life is a testament to compounding success. In 2016 when I started Chef Diamond and Friends kids' series with my first book "Chef Diamond Goes Grocery Shopping" I knew I was committing to an entire new brand that I would need to focus on in order to make it successful. Once I committed to making it successful, I began getting diverse ideas on how to make it better. After selling coloring books I realized I had nothing else to sell, this prompted me to create more products and services in order to generate the numbers that would make the business viable. With that vision in mind, I set a goal to create 75 books with 3-6 characters that others could relate to.

I did the numbers and I realized if I sold one million copies of my 75 books at $10 minimum, I would generate $750 million alone in book sales which is basic math. In 2020 right before the pandemic hit I was preparing to teach more kids how to cook and decided to create our own chef hats, knives, aprons and culinary tools into a culinary kit. The kit would cost $125 and if we sold 10,000 kits we could generate 1.25 million dollars. I came back to my reality at the times when all of these products didn't exist and I had to create them all.

It may be a different industry in your case, different gifts or even different products and services but remember the power of compounding success. The key to achieving more in life is by doing more and becoming more. The numbers above were for just products but we also offered cooking classes to kids and together we are on the path to reaching our ultimate goal while making a difference and operating in the sweet spot at all times. Remember, anything is possible when you believe in yourself. Create a plan, commit to the plan, take action and never give up.

Make success your video game, learn accounting and finance so you can effectively manage money throughout the process. Be willing and ready to take risks, you may not win on your first try but don't give up – keep going.

NOTES

LEVEL 7

BE UNSTOPPABLE

Success is your video game, not anyone else's!

By now, it is my prayer that you have grown in understanding success on a deeper level. With this new found insight I want you to wake up every day with your head held high knowing who you are, where you are going and what you need to do in order to get there. This book is just the beginning of your journey so I commend you for taking the time to read it, the next step is intentionally applying what you have read.

What's stopping you from closing this book and going full force until you reach your goals? It doesn't matter if it takes 2 years, 5 years or 20 years.

I spoke about being conditioned for success and that starts with your mind and will power. There is a book titled "As a man thinketh and as a woman thinketh" which clearly shows how success first begins in the mind.

I want you to be successful but do you want to be successful? My desire for you to win in life is not enough. You must make the decision to win now despite the odds. Decide that nothing will stop you from achieving your goals in life. Be unstoppable! Don't do anything illegal but focus on identifying everything that is currently stopping you and could potentially stop you from reaching your goals.

List 5 things that are currently stopping you from reaching your goals?

1. _____

2. _____

3. _____

4. _____

5. _____

List 5 things that could stop you from reaching your goals in the future? Think about the future obstacles based on your desires.

1. _____

2. _____

3. _____

4. _____

5. _____

MAD SCIENTIST

Your journey will make you a strong individual. There will be moments of isolation where you need to sit alone and plan, think and strategize before bringing others into the discussion. Embrace those moments. Do not be afraid to be alone with yourself and your thoughts. It is in those moments that everything comes together.

When you look at some of the greatest individuals in the world and watch them perform, it nearly seems unimaginable to many but remember they are mad scientists as well.

Example: The great leaders in sports or any other arena spend hours and decades studying their crafts, studying the competition and eventually the time comes for them to share what they have done with the world and everyone is amazed. You are on your way to greatness! I repeat, you are on your way to greatness. You have the formula to becoming successful, don't let anything stop you.

OVERCOMING LACK OF SUPPORT

What happens if no one supports your dreams for 5+ years? Will you give up? Will you abandon the mission?

If you can adopt the mindset of achieving your goals because it is your destiny and not just because of the applause of men or the fame you may get, then you will become unstoppable. When you learn to execute at a high level with or without anyone watching, you become unstoppable.

Story:

Currently, I've written 9 books on success and developed 35 books for my Chef Diamond and Friends series. I remember checking my metrics during the process to find that 2000 people had visited my website when I released my first book but only 2 people purchased a book. I was discouraged but over time I realized that I was marketing to the wrong people and every time I released a new product or service I would only share it with those who were around me instead of getting it in front of the people who would love, appreciate and purchase my products and services.

Even if you get discouraged in the moment, don't let it hold you back. I never allowed the discouraging moments to stop me from pursuing my ultimate goal. I am proud of my team and all that we have accomplished so far and all that we will accomplish in the future.

THE EXPECTATION TO BREAKTHROUGH

There are two scriptures in the Bible I want you to hold on to throughout your journey.

> *"Do not despise these small beginnings, for the Lord rejoices to see the work begin, to see the plumb line in Zerubbabel's hand."*
> *(Zechariah 4:10)*

Do not despise small beginning because you won't always be small. When you are small and come across others who have built multi-million dollar businesses, I want it to inspire you not intimidate you. Imagine believing and working diligently towards a goal for 20 years and it finally becomes a reality, how would you feel? Now, imagine desiring something but not working towards it and 40 years later you are still talking about the ideas you had 40 years ago. Compare the feelings, which would you rather have, that of accomplishment or that of regret?

Start small and build everything that comes to you. As you begin the process, things will get clearer and you will become a person worthy of all you desire in life.

> *"And let us not be weary in well doing: for in due season we shall reap, if we faint not."*
> *(Galatians 6:9)*

Sometimes, your breakthrough doesn't occur according to the planned time that's why you need the mental strength to keep putting in the work, believing that it will work out. Do not get weary in pursuing your goals and dreams especially if you run out of money or have other obstacles come your way, pause and then come back to it tomorrow. Rome wasn't built in one day.

If you love success and you are ready to begin your journey to success visit www.McNultyInternational.com and sign up for the Success Club. The Success Club is a group of likeminded individuals that are committed to reaching their goals in life. We currently support three clubs:

- The High School Success Club

- The College Success Club

- The Adult Success Club

All of these clubs include access to our learning portal, courses, success club community and success circle group meetings where we come together to study success.

There are opportunities for one-on-one Coaching and Mentoring as well.

In the meantime, there are some additional materials to aid your success at www.ShopMcNulty.com.

- For young men, get a copy of How to Become a Successful Young Man (Book & Workbook).

- For young women, get a copy of How to Become a Successful Young Woman (Book & Workbook).

- For adults you can get a copy of Success Recovery.

If you have been blessed by this book, please, write a 5 star review on our McNulty International Facebook, Google or Yelp profile. It would mean the world to me to see the impact in real-time as you begin your journey to success. I thank you in advance and wish you much success on your journey and remember, success is your video-game!

NOTES

NOTES

ABOUT THE AUTHOR

Diamond McNulty is an entrepreneur and author of several books, his most noted being "How to Become a Successful Young Man". He was born and raised in the Cabrini Green Housing projects on the north side of Chicago, Illinois. Despite growing up surrounded by gang violence and limited opportunities, McNulty has achieved tremendous success at a young age. He has founded and grown five successful companies, including winning competitions like Steve Harvey's Act Like A Success and is now the board chairman of The Chicago Youth Programs, the same organization that provided him access and opportunities to success. www.ChicagoYouthPrograms.org

Diamond McNulty believes in others as much as he believes in himself. Diamond is passionate about helping others succeed and empowering the next generation to strive for greatness. He is also an active executive board member for various schools and nonprofit organizations. Diamond prides himself on being very active inside the community and making a difference. All of his endeavors have the same underlying mission, to help others grow through literacy, understand the journey to success, and motivate others via speaking.

McNulty's personal motto is "Take over the world," and he is passionate about sharing his experience and knowledge with others, especially through mentoring children. Inspired by his mother's resilience and driven by his passion for making a difference, McNulty is constantly pursuing new ventures and ideas. He is on the road to becoming a billionaire philanthropist and positively impacting the lives of others with his success. McNulty's energy, passion, and faith makes him an individual to watch in the world of business and beyond.

Learn more or book Diamond McNulty to speak at

www.DiamondMcNulty.com

Made in United States
Troutdale, OR
08/08/2024

21853986R00051